Something in the Potato Room

Heather Cousins

Especially for my sisters,
Erin and Kaitlin.

Selected by Patricia Smith

2009 Kore Press first book award winner

Something in the Potato Room

Heather Cousins

Kore Press, Inc.
Tucson, Arizona USA
www.korepress.org

ISBN 13   978-1-888553-39-0

Design by Sally Geier
Cover design by Christina Louise Smith

Type set in Cochin.

The passage on page 58 contains found text from *The Will To Believe* (1896) by William James and the "forward" by Ellis R. Kerley, Ph.D. in *Essentials in Forensic Anthropolgy* (1979) by T.D. Stewart, M.D.

"Electricity Experiment." © Mary Evans Picture Library.

G is a Girl. Stories and Rhymes for Children, Part I, 1838. From the collection of Old Sturbridge Village, Sturbridge, Massachusetts.

Contents

PART I

In which, as in ancient thought, North is the land
of the dead, in that direction do the dead set out.

When nervous, I drew
crosses. Not Latin, but
Maltese. Arms large and
blunt. Equal in length
and width, narrowing
towards the center. I
was the first one out
when the lunch break
ladies played whist. Fidg-
et their prials. Their em-
pire quarters. Sitting and
staring at their crotches
and spades. My saliva
tasted like pennies—like
the head on beer. I read
that this can be a symp-
tom. Of heart disease. Or
anemia.

Typing. Copying. Balancing the museum accounts. Some days there wasn't much work. I often sat at my desk and wished that my fingernails would grow. I searched the Internet for holiday-specific screen savers. A haunted house with an audio clip. Eek. A Christmas tree that decorated and undecorated itself. One afternoon, after exploding confetti and the year bouncing around the screen to the bleats of noisemakers, Dr. Paul asked me if I would clean the conference room. He directed me to the rags and spray bottles in the supply closet. Gave me a key. Inside the conference room, I went to work on cookie crumbs and old coffee rings. While I was scrubbing, one of the curators walked by. The door had a glass window. Beveled. He stopped and studied me through it. He opened the door. Asked me who I was. Whether I was allowed in there.

In April, Dr. Paul recommended a vacation. Had I begun to typo? To miscalculate? Had he noticed the spit-cleaning of the conference room? Perhaps it was the new smell. I had switched shampoos. I was now infused with lavender and cherry blossoms.

I rented a room at a seaside motel, "The Breezes." Stucco with a kidney-shaped pool. When—in the history of man—did we begin to refer to that which is "kidney-shaped"? The ocean was only two blocks away. Every morning, I took a white motel towel and a copy of *Heart of Darkness* to the beach. I was reading it for the fourth time. For the fourth time, Marlow sits on the carcass of the riverboat. For the fourth time, he has a fever. For the fourth time, one can't live with one's finger everlastingly on one's pulse.

Last day at the beach.
My kneecaps were two
hot stones. I was apply-
ing sunblock when I saw
the fish being rolled in the
breakers. Pale. Bloated. I
walked past two children
who had been building a
giant woman out of sand,
carving—just then—the
V between her legs. I
walked into the shell line,
where the mole crabs
bubbled and ran with ev-
ery wave. The fish was
metal, covered with small
clams. It wasn't a fish. It
was some sort of missile.
A torpedo. A wayward. A
slipshod.

I leaned down to touch it, gently daub with the tip of my finger. But the voices of the children almost knocked me over. They raced under my legs. Splashed in the shallows. Little otters. Soon a small crowd. A man in a dune buggy and uniform. A captain. A cavalry.

They evacuated the beach. Half an hour later, we heard the boom of their careful detonation. Sonic. Trembling. In my excitement, I must have left my book behind. When they allowed us back, there was a crater in the sand. Marlow was everywhere—stuck in the wet sand, fluttering in the breeze, some of the pages with burnt corners.

It wasn't a fish.

I went back to work.

Another secretary asked
why I didn't go to the
beach.

I told her I did.

But you didn't get any
sun, she said.

There was a problem with the donation box. It sat in the foyer of the museum. Clear plastic, with a slit in the top. You could watch your dollars and cents drop. A black bear loomed over it, his head-sized paws threatening visitors to contribute. He was stuffed. But still dangerous.

Dr. Paul always recommended that a good "base" of cash be left on the bottom of the donation box, even after it had been emptied: "People won't donate, if they don't think anyone else has." Dr. Paul believed that people were social animals. Liked to work in packs.

We took turns emptying the donation box. Last time, I counted out five hundred seventeen dollars. Returned one hundred and twenty. I made sure, just like Dr. Paul always said, to leave a few big bills right at the top.

This week, it was Sandy's turn.

She only found eighty dollars—all ones.

9

Dr. Paul called me into his office. He asked how much money I had left in the box: "How much money did you leave in the box?" When I told him three times, he asked back three times: "Are you sure?" He tugged on his earlobe. I asked if I was going to be fired. He said I wasn't—unless there was a reason for me to be fired? My jaw dropped and my mouth made a large O—big enough to stick an apple in.

I had to make something happen. I had to change my life. I called a realtor. A woman with fuzzy hair: a dandelion's gossamer ball. Achenes, waiting to be wished upon.

She showed me the market. She asked me personal questions about my savings account. Shortly thereafter, I made a down payment on a large house. The color of lips and toenails.

Because I bought everything—my books, my clothing, my Victorian cutlery collection—from the Presbyterian Thrift, I had a small nest egg. Fertilized. Wouldn't this make it better? Wasn't I just "stuck in a rut"? A standard pattern? A Federalist? A Simple? A Plain?

The new house had a smell. Palpable. A pink fog. Low-toned buzzing. Something familiar. I worried through my memories. Poodle fur. Impetigo. A summer evening as a young girl, when I had stepped spinningwise in cold, bare feet upon a luna moth. Dewy wings in the night grass. Like crushing a Chinese lantern.

In the night grass.

PART II

In which it is all moving underneath.

On the balcony of the
new house, I looked down
at the dandelion back-
yard and my white wrist,
where, as a child, petals
had been rubbed. Yel-
low. Saffron. Curry. If it
were love skin. But mine
wasn't. I sized up the
distance to the ground:
twenty feet? thirty? How
many toes? If I jumped,
would they roll off my
feet like marbles?

15

The house wasn't enough. I went to an animal shelter. Cage after cage of barking, white muzzles. Shepherds and retrievers. Flecked and golden hairs floated in the corridor. They had bowls of water and empty. What if I forgot? What if I didn't have the energy? I often slept twelve hours a night.

In the cat room, noses and paws pushed out between silver bars. Globes of fur and skin. Humans can grow tumors with teeth and hair. Cells that want to make a face. A new person.

My throat worried me,
and I was light-headed.
"I might have diphtheria,"
I said, calling into work.
I put on a sock hat, pink
pom-pommed, and began
to crack eggs.

After an omelet, I timed
my palpitations. When
they subsided, I decided
I might as well do some
unpacking. I tackled the
collection: silverware,
sterling and plated, sealed
into Johnny Walker box-
es. I had found the per-
fect squares at the liquor
store. The collections had
grown too large; some of
the lesser pieces would
have to be moved to the
basement—a   low-ceil-
inged room, with small
windows: half-ground,
half-sky.

If there were a tornado,
I would be safe. I would
crouch, arms over head,
in the southwest corner.

The boxes left drag trails
on the long-unswept floor.
I hurried through the
dust and mites, singing
"The Bear Went Over the
Mountain." The vibra-
tions of my voice shook
the spider webs and the
spiders stopped moving
their eight legs. While
pushing with my foot
a box of soup spoons, I
found, behind the stairs,
a small wooden door.
Corbelled and planked.
There was a lock, but the
lock was rusted through.

The door opened. Crumbs
of rotted wood stuck to
my hand. I threw them
over my left shoulder like
salt. My eyes adjusted to
the darkness, expecting
roots. Earwigs. Sack-
ing. But something else
was there. A horrible. A
squatter. A chief of the
Inner Station.

I bolted upstairs, fright-
ened that he might some-
how come after. I dug
myself into the laundry
hamper. Rabbit breath-
ing in sweatshirts and
white underwear. (Prac-
tical. Good Girl under-
wear.) My nervous fin-
gers found a used dryer
sheet. Mountain Fresh.
I rubbed my cheeks with
it. Was he dangerous?
Diseased?

PART III

In which he turns and the sun turns and the spoons turn.

I told myself: Call the police. I imagined the conversation: Hello officer? Come quickly! Yes ma'am, we're on our way. With the news anchor and her pearl-buttoned blouse.

They would take my squatter in their squad car. They would count his bones. They would assemble. On black cloth. Photograph-ready. Archival. Click, click. Men with monogrammed handkerchiefs would scramble to the courthouse to look through yellow, secret-smelling papers. Dr. Paul would have his handkerchief, WJP tucked in his breast pocket, laughing and sniffing, holding cracked newspaper against his white upper lip.

I pulled a piece of string across the fourth stair, ankle height, and laced three jingle bells through it, then duct-taped each end to the white walls. I applauded myself. Not everyone would have thought of the jingle bells, nor had them on hand. I locked my bedroom door, crawled into bed, and buried myself in stuffy hot.

I couldn't sleep, picturing him curled up behind that small wooden door. How long had he been? The bells never rang, never even trembled. And I didn't get any rashes or fevers. When morning came, I stayed in bed. I didn't want to go to the museum. I didn't want to be in a place where everything is behind glass and says "Please do not touch."

The vibrations.

Over coffee, not at work, I read an article in the Free Press about the year's Pulitzer Prize winners. Ten thousand dollars to Ms. Marcus for her "masterful stories about patients, families and physicians that illuminated the often unseen world of cancer survivors."

I began to think there was a reason for my discovery. He could be my project. My salvage. I would find out everything. An agent. A digger. Primum mobile.

I put on a wool skirt and went to the courthouse. I brought a notebook and pencils. I brought a roll of quarters and an expanding file folder. There were computers and microfiche viewers. I rolled the word silently on my tongue: microfiche, microfiche, microfiche.

More of what there was: Electric outlets with surprised faces. Cords, wires, and strings. Heavy wooden tables with waxy varnish. Troffer ceiling lights. Fibrous carpet, thin and flat. Army-colored filing cabinets in formation. Names and dates. Newspaper photographs. Sepia. Curling. Brittle.

But there weren't any answers. Or even hypotheses. Was my method wrong? My skills? I had expected to come home with names and dates, pinned to my blouse like medals.

I took a peppermint star brite from a bowl at the sign-out desk. Unwrapped the stiff cellophane. Sucked hard. Crunched.

I walked down the base-
ment stairs to the wooden
door—a door for an old
woman, back bent, ossi-
fied in burden. I peered
inside the small, earthen
room. A dark, crumbling,
walk-in. Perhaps it had
been used for keeping ice.
Or vegetables. A potato
room. He lay in a corner.
Watching him, I felt pink
and full of skin.

What I wanted to do most
in the museum was touch.
To have that authority,
which no visitor is per-
mitted. I often stood in
front of the glass, think-
ing about the artifacts.
The basket of wool cards
and sewing shuttles. The
Ojibway arrowheads. The
tray of Civil War buttons:
one with a gouge across
its eagle. I would imagine
the original owner—hair
color, rotted tooth, mud-
dy blanket, bear dreams,
final vision: shuddering
birds, winged readies
dropping from the sky.

PART IV

In which the pleasant is proved peninsular.

After three days of calling in sick, I returned to the museum. My coworkers inquired about my health. "I just hope it's not cancer," I said. I splashed water on my face in the ladies room and didn't dry with a paper towel, but let the drips roll down my neck and wrists. Around noon, Dr. Paul stood behind my desk. Looming. A reconnaissance balloon. A zeppelin. "I had all of the secretaries take a typing test while you were gone," he said, handing me a CD. "Put this in the computer. It will let us know how fast you type." My fingertips flattened into suction cups.

I returned.

I went to the library on
Auburn Rd. A forest.
Books at my feet, belly,
and head. Higher than
I could reach. Hun-
dreds. Thousands. Inside
their skins, letters buzz-
ing: molecules knock-
ing together: chains of
mutuality.

Harvesting: I checked out
1.) *Essentials of Forensic
Anthropology* by Thomas
Dale Stewart 2.) *Dead Men
Do Tell Tales* by William
R. Maples and Michael
Brumming and 3.) *Days
of the Cutting Edge: History
of the Perry Robeson
Cutlery Company* by Clark
T. Rice.

Back home, I put on gloves. I searched for signs of violence. Cut marks. Char. A broken hyoid bone. I examined the matted fibers. Flannel and wool sock. The data went into a blue notebook, with space left for diagrams and charts. I hummed a theme song. After measuring his femur, I took off the gloves. There was a reason he looked so helpless. Estimated standing height: four-and-a-half feet. Twenty five teeth. I wiggled a small one.

Dr. Paul said that I was the slowest typist in the office. "Thirty-five words a minute is not acceptable," he said, the pores of his skin opening and closing like thousands of little baby mouths.

It was cold in the potato room, so I brought down a quilt. A Basket Pattern. I spread it out on top of him so that only his head peeked out. Oyster head. Glowing.

Thousands of little baby mouths.

PART V

In which there is a sudden, golden sound.

"It's these computers," I tried to explain to Dr. Paul. "I learned to type on a Smith Corona."

Dr. Paul handed me an application for Keyboarding I. It was being offered at East Lansing C.C. Name, the application demanded. Birth date. Highest level of education. I folded it into an origami crane and tucked it in a jar of yogurt-covered raisins.

Virginia, the secretary with pink frost lips, passed by my desk. "Hello space cadet," she said and knocked her fist on the top of my head. "You want to play whist with us at lunch?" Whist had been my idea. I had pointed it out in Hoyle's Rules. But I couldn't catch on.

"You'll figure it out one of these days." Virginia said.

"I already figured it out," I said.

She rolled her pink frost lips and winked. Stitches of crow's feet deepened around her eyes.

Underneath the quilt, a
red vine was growing.
Slithering. Crawling up
his arm. Sneaky-snake.
Leaky ache. Should I
bring down the shears?
The trimming blades? Or
was it the sort of weed
that needed to be uproot-
ed—dug out, its white
heart held in my palm?

I was becoming a library regular. My laminated card had milky bends on the corners. Ricketed from transparent to opaque. The books made me feel like breathing. They still maintained their plant magic. Carbon dioxide. Oxygen. Respiration.

I checked out: 1.) *The National Audobon Society Field Guide to North American Mushrooms* 2.) *Introduction to Fungi* by John Webster and Roland Weber 3.) *The Homeowner's Guide to Mold* by Michael A. Pugliese and 4.) *Spoon River Anthology*, although I knew it wasn't really about spoons.

As the librarian scanned my card, I noticed a sign above her head: Shelver wanted. I pictured myself threading quietly between the stacks, wearing glasses on a chain. I could push the book trolley, learn the song of its wheels. Or hide in a quiet corner, nibbling crackers, vibrating with the letters, words, sentences.

G g GIRL.

G is a Girl,
　With a quiet look;
She sits in a chair,
　And reads in a book.

I pictured myself.

Yeasts? Mildews? Rusts?
I flipped through the
chapters of the guides. I
was studying a photo of
a red lichen, when there
was movement. Periph-
eral. A quick flick of the
wrist. As if someone had
tugged it with a string.
I closed the book. My
hands felt padded, paw-
like, huge. Leaning over
his scaffolding, I whis-
pered, "Do it again."

In the potato room

the tubers

are supposed to stay

cold

don't sprout

don't open

their hundred

thousand

eyes an exhale

a lung beat

the wet fog

of one

white

breath.

He's growing in the
humid

under the blankets

a live thing

a beating.

What grows from the
buried? Roots

are supposed to shoot
down

green.

What has been placed
here

has been placed here

to DORMANT.
to STILL.
to STULLIFY.

But it hasn't.
Pink and red and pink.

PART VI

In which, at the black bottom, many fish glow.

Holding a can of north-
ern beans at the grocery
store, I was approached
by an old man in a jelly-
smeared cardigan. Prox-
emics. Haptics. Chiron-
omy. "How much?" the
old man begged through
ancient, chalk lips. The
smear of jelly seemed to
spread out, fattening. A
new stomach. "Seventy-
nine cents," I said. He
nodded. His breath was
the breath of shrouds,
thin veins, tubing. His
breath was the breath of
steel tables, wire, brown
velvet. Suction. Trocars.
Doves and lilies.

I cleaned out my desk at the museum. There wasn't much to take. A pot of paperwhites. A green mug. A bottle of ibuprofen and a sheet of Sudafed, the little red gems sealed in foil. I had told Dr. Paul that morning, and asked him if I should wait the requisite two weeks. He shook his head. His exhale blew the bangs off my forehead.

The boy made sounds, his jaw bones grinding together. Clam shells. Door hinges. Two sticks trying to make fire. Passing my hand in front of his mandible, a burst of warm. I curled up next to him, and we groaned together.

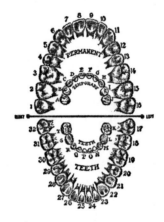

What grows from the buried?

It seemed as if it hurt—
the coming-back-to-life.
Like frozen toes in hot
water. The ache and
shiver of blood breaking
from its sluggish sleep.
A million square cells
growing—opening like
eyelids, like shutters whip-
ping up from windows.
New apartments. Noisy.
Cranky.

I held him. Like sailors
hold oars. Like the starv-
ing hold bread. Like boy
scouts hold knots. He was
pointy and full of scuttles.
He smelled of mushrooms
and placenta. It filled the
small room. Coated us.
An oily dust. My hair and
eyelashes were full of it.

His jaw began to slide,
as if waxed. His bones
were covered in spongy
pink. Pillows. Sachets.
He had a tongue, which
he stuck out at me. It
trembled from the middle
of his black mouth hole. A
streamer. A hose.

His first word was *nrnnnn*. Infantile. Lisped. I clapped my hands and brought down flash-cards. Baseball. Fish. Xylophone. Zebra. After every new sound, I fed him out of a jar of peanut butter. Little nibbles from my finger.

A cave of. Crumbling
brick work. A dirty.
A black. A boundless.
Inklike. Hours. Days.
He was sprouting. Full
sentences. His body
blossomed like a tree.
Buds knotting bone.
"Look at the head of
your femur," I pointed.
"It's growing a flower."

I asked him: when he
lived, how he died. I
asked him, my palms
melting-molting, if he
had seen God. He shook
his wibble-wobble head.
His new lips—puffed,
sticky—tacky-trembled.
"Beebah mmmbaaahhhh,"
he said.

The language may have been tonal. Like Chinese.

Connected by a chain of events the word entity means any physical object or phenomenon something that fills a void completely and satisfyingly it explains in detail how he or she goes about reconstructing the biological nature of an individual there are laws which govern the need to explain, predict, and master phenomena resulting in the construction of models of reality and disagreement between the scientists and the philosophers and the poets truth envisaged aptitudinem ad extorquendum certum assensum our passional nature in conflict with or in harmony with our intellectual grounds.

PART VII

In which the dead arise and walk again.
The dead are quiet walkers.

I brought down the best
of the collection. Showed
him my cusps, my cap-
pers: nickel tongs shaped
like eagle's claws; a silver
sugar sifter—BLM mono-
grammed on the handle;
and, last but not least, the
rare 19th century melon
baller.

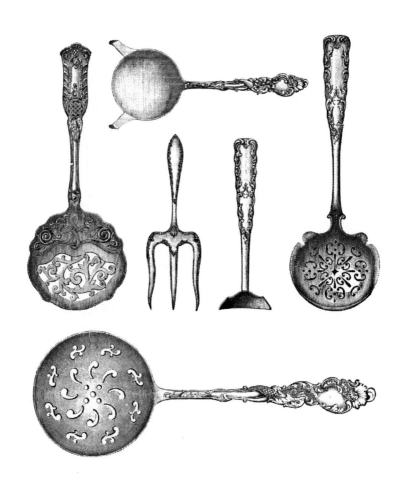

My cusps, my cappers.

His eyeballs were milky
in the Cimmerian dark-
ness. In the center of the
floor, I had placed a ker-
osene lamp. Sometimes
we made shapes in the
shadows. I showed him a
bird. And a barking dog.
In turn, with his sharp
bones and new tendons,
he made squirrel. Heron.
Crocodile with teeth.

"It's soft here," I told him, "and I like to forget." We were eating chunky soup. He looked at me with his eyes: they were growing in blue—arctic. "Heh Neh Owh," he said, picking out from his bowl a cube of carrot and tucking it into his soft new cheek. I nodded my head and added the words to my blue-notebook dictionary.

A message. A warn-
ing. All signs pointed.
The fetid turning of
my skin. The loss—in-
explicable—of a can of
wax beans. The urgent
banging upstairs. At the
entrance to the main.

I woke up after a nap. I
don't know what time it
was. In the potato room,
it was always crepuscu-
lar. Twilight. Last light.
Thwill. It was empty. Toll-
ing. He was disappeared.
Gone. Gone. Gone. Gone.
Gone. Gone

I called and called. We
had so many more things
to discover. To unearth.
I yearned to rub his man-
dible. I searched every-
where. The dishes were
cold, the pillows were hot.
I opened the little door
for the first time in weeks.
Light wafted in. A point-
ed pain between the eyes.
Lake up one's nose. Sharp
water-on-bone headache.

I closed it again.

The urgent banging.

Any physical theory is always provisional new and improved theories should explain all the observations of the old theory in addition to the new set of facts pluralitas non est ponenda sine necessitate "Oh necessitate," I said with my face against the cold dirt floor.

My skin is pale. The color of moonlight. Life doesn't stay still, and death doesn't stay still either. In the corner of the potato room, after crawling around and around, I found a pearl of bone. He must have left it behind. His body filled in flesh for the missing piece. Or grew a new. When I hold it up to my ear, I hear a small sound. Clinking. Like silver.

I am waiting for him. Or for me. I'm not sure anymore. My head hurts, and I have to lie down. I like to fold the thin pieces of the quilt around my fingers. The earwigs are whispering. The beetles chew the fat. I think pretty soon it will make sense to me. I'll know everything. I'll touch it. At last—everything.

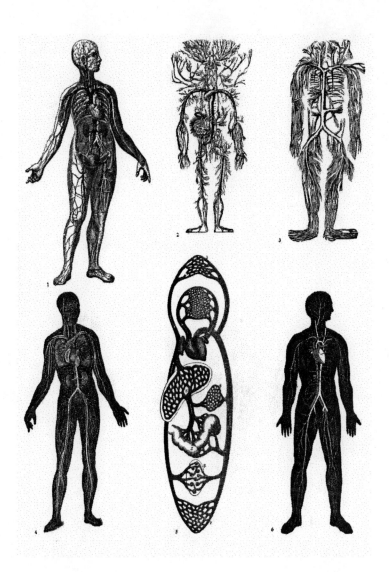

Acknowledgments

My sincerest thanks to Lisa Bowden, Christina Smith, and the rest of Kore Press for bringing this book into being. Many thanks to Patricia Smith for choosing my manuscript. To my peers and mentors at the University of Georgia, especially Judith Ortiz Cofer and the writers in her spring 2006 graduate workshop for their helpful critiques. Special thanks to Andy Frazee, Matt Forsythe, John Spiers, John Woods, Danielle Pafunda, Kirsten Kaschock, and Kaitlin Matesich for their careful readings, suggestions, and enthusiasm. To Robin Wharton and the Georgia Lawyers for the Arts for counsel on illustration copyright. To Matthew Boyd and *Staccato* for publishing an early effort. To Heather Price and Danielle Sellers for their friendship and writing advice. And, finally, to Mom, Dad, Gavin, Kaitlin, Erin, and David for their love and support.

Heather Cousins is the winner of the 2009 Kore Press First Book Award. She received a BA in Anthropology from Bryn Mawr College in 2001, an MA in The Writing Seminars at Johns Hopkins University in 2002, and a PhD in Creative Writing in Spring 2009 from the University of Georgia. She was a Finalist for The Yalobusha Review Yellowwood Poetry Prize in 2009. She grew up in Bear Lake, Michigan and currently lives in Monroe, Georgia.

Kore Press expresses gratitude to those who helped make the Kore Press First Book Award possible: The Tucson-Pima Arts Council, The Arizona Commission on the Arts, through appropriations from the Arizona State Legislature and the National Endowment for the Arts, the manuscript readers, the judge, and all the writers who submitted their work each year.

Previous first book award winners: Jennifer Barber for *Rigging the Wind*, selected by Jane Miller; Deborah Fries for *Various Modes of Departure*, selected by Carolyn Forché; Elline Lipkin for *The Errant Thread*, selected by Eavan Boland; Sandra Lim for *Loveliest Grotesque*, selected by Marilyn Chin; Spring Ulmer for *Benjamin's Spectacles*, selected by Sonia Sanchez; and Holly Iglesias for *Souvenirs of a Shrunken World*, selected by Harryette Mullen.